THE SCRIPTURE IN THE STARS

MICHAEL LEDO

ISBN1451554346
EAN-139781451554342
Primary Category: Religion / Christianity / General

INTRODUCTION

I have discovered the secret of the ages, the astrology code of the Bible. Many of the stories in the Bible play out in the constellations. Anyone who has read the work of E.W. Bullinger's *The Witness of the Stars* is familiar with how the Bible relates to the constellations.

Bullinger's work concentrated mostly on the New Testament. My work is mostly concerned on the Old Testament, although I do make references to the New Testament and at times my work contradicts that of Bullinger's.

This book is part of a larger work, *On Earth as it is in Heaven, The Cosmic Roots of the Bible.* I have arranged subject matter differently in this book, listing by constellations instead of stories. I do digress from this formula slightly toward the end by combining constellations to make the story flow smoother.

My previous work was filled with end notes with documentation of sources, so much so, it was painful to read. I have eliminated those sources for this text in order to make it a more pleasant and inspirational read. For those who desire those sources, I will refer you to my aforesaid tome.

What this book does NOT take into consideration is the origin of the Bible, or what the original Bible text may have looked like. That made up a large portion of *On Earth as it is in Heaven.* I will not be discussing that here. This book is for those who just want to see the baby without hearing about the labor pains.

In addition to curious believers, this book would be of interest to astronomers as a field guide in locating Bible stories in God's heavens.

There were four beliefs of ancient Bible interpreters:

1) There was a cryptic or secret text contained within the Bible.
2) The Bible applied to their time, even though it was written centuries earlier.
3) The Bible was inerrant, even though the contradictions were apparent.
4) The Bible was divinely inspired, even though they were aware that men wrote and altered the text.

In fact, modern scholars are so self-righteous in their knowledge they proclaim, "The ancient interpreters did not know more than we do about the biblical world or about history or about Bible authors. They knew less."

If we accepted for the sake of argument that the Bible has an astrological or cosmic content used for prophecy, then all of the above statements would be true. Bible contradictions were astrological stories that applied to different peoples, places, and ages.

The idea of biblical astrology is not widely accepted. I originally planned to take what are considered New Age authors of the late nineteenth century and repackage their ideas in light of new discoveries. I had trouble getting started and shelved the project for four years.

In 2002 I returned to the project. I realized I had been looking at the Bible all wrong. I needed to do some editing of the text to bring out the astronomical/astrological material. Armed with the infinite power and wisdom of the Internet, I felt I could breeze through the subject matter, having indexed libraries at my fingertips. As I discovered, it was not quite that easy. I ended up breaking much new ground.

As it turned out, the Bible stories were not just a haphazard collection of cosmic myths, but rather a contiguous story of the constellations. The final proof came when the remaining story of David was able to aptly coincide with the few unused remnant constellations of Sagittarius, Scorpio, and Ara. There were also smoking guns along the way, such as the story of Passover lining up with the vernal equinox; Joshua stopping the sun in the sky at a place of a supernova, which lit up the ancient sky as a nighttime sun; the winter solstice lining up with the blinding of the solar figure Samson; and the autumnal equinox coinciding with the death of Uriah. This type of coincidence just does not happen.

Contents

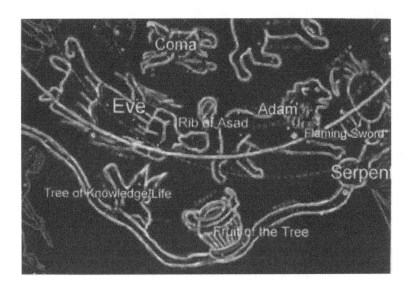

LEO

Leo is Adam. The Hebrew etymology of the word Adam indicates a root meaning "to have a red face. The red star Regulus marks the heart of the lion and in ancient times designated the summer solstice. This was the beginning of the calendar year and of creation in the Bible.

Adam was the ancient form of Leo, called Asad. Based on the Arabic names of various stars related to the parts of a lion, it is held that there once existed a large lion constellation which incorporated several constellations, among which were Cancer, Leo, Virgo, and Libra. Ptolemy and the later Arab astronomers were responsible for the split into various constellations of the original Asad, as it appeared in the initial zodiac.

Some of the stars of Virgo were originally assigned to Asad. These stars, which would be a rib of the lion, comprised the constellation Virgo. The star Zavijava was known as *Warak al Asad,"* the "Lion's Haunches." This was the rib taken from Adam to make his wife.

Genesis 2:21 *And YHWH caused a deep sleep to fall upon the man, and he slept; and he took one of his ribs, and closed up the flesh instead thereof: 22 and the rib, which YHWH had taken from the man, he made a woman, and brought her unto the man.*

When the constellation of Leo underwent its major overhaul by the Greeks, this made the story of Adam and the rib inaccurate in the astral sense. The rabbis apparently were aware of the true origin of Adam as Asad because they created a story to fit the new constellation. Instead of a rib, it was Adam's tail that was used to create Eve. Upon examining the current constellations of Leo and Virgo, we find it is the tail of the lion that joins with the head of the woman. In the tail there is a star the Hebrews named Sarcam, which literally means "the joining." This tail would become a reinterpretation of the rib YHWH took from Adam to make his wife.

VIRGO

Virgo, as mentioned above was Eve. The constellation also symbolized Sarah when she was in Egypt and the virgin Mary of the New Testament. This sign was associated with the planet Venus. Bethlehem, which means "House of Bread" was associated with this constellation. The star Spica in Virgo was Eden. It was also known as Emuku Tin tir Ki, the Might of the Abode of Life.

HYDRA

Hydra is a serpent located at the feet of Leo and Virgo. It was the serpent in the Garden of Eden. It located low in the horizon, near the ground. This accounts for the curse in Genesis: 3:14

So the Lord God said to the serpent: "Because you have done this, You are cursed more than all cattle, And more than every beast of the field; On your belly you shall go, And you shall eat dust All the days of your life. 15 And I will put enmity Between you and the woman, And between your seed and her Seed; He shall bruise your head, And you shall bruise His heel."

CORVUS THE RAVEN

Corvus is the tree of knowledge. It is also the raven or crow that is released in the flood stories. Genesis 8:7 *And he sent forth a raven...*

CRATER THE CUP

Crater is the fruit of the Tree of Life and the fruit of the Tree of Knowledge. It is also the legendary Holy Grail. Drinking of the cup is said to give one knowledge and eternal life.

COMA

Coma was originally part of the lion's tail. In Egypt, the constellation was pictured as a mother and child. It represented hope for a nation. In the Old Testament it was the promise God made to Abraham that his children would become God's chosen.

In the New Testament it is the child prodigy; Jesus in the temple dazzling the wise rabbis with his wisdom. Coma coupled with nearby Virgo provides the prophecy in Isa. 7:14

Therefore the Lord himself shall give you a sign: Behold a virgin shall conceive, and bear a son, and shall call his name Immanuel.

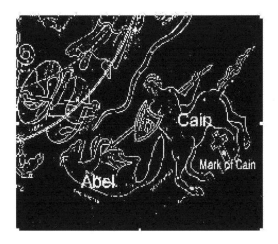

CENTAURUS

Centaurus is Cain. The word Cain mean "to strike fast" with a spear. The constellations as well as the name of Cain informs us of how Cain killed Abel. In the New Testament Cain would be the centurion who spears Christ in the side. It is also Pilate. The name Pilate means "armed with a spear." This is a natural allusion to Centaurus, killing his victim with spear in hand.

LUPUS THE VICTIM

As you may have guessed, this is Abel. In the New Testament it would represent Jesus on the Cross. When their blood was spilt on the ground, an earthquake happened on both occasions. This is symbolic of the nearness to the horizon of the constellation.

SOUTHERN CROSS

The Southern Cross was the cross of Jesus, still visible in Jerusalem in 33 A.D. In the Old Testament it was the mark of Cain. The Jewish tradition claims the "Mark of Cain" was the letter Teth translated as Tau. This letter looks similar to the Southern Cross.

These constellations would have been visible right before sunrise in Jerusalem in 33 AD.

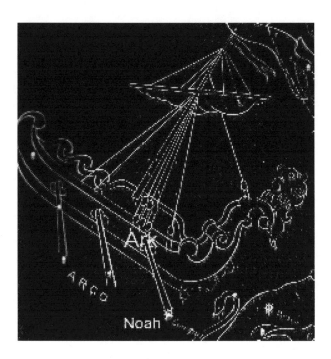

ARGO

Argo the ship is Noah's ark. Canopus, the brightest star in Argo is known as "the navigator." The ark landed on a nearby star Hadar, which means "ground."

THE DOVE OF NOAH

The Dove of Noah is a nearby constellation. It is of modern nomenclature and is in an apt location for its designation.

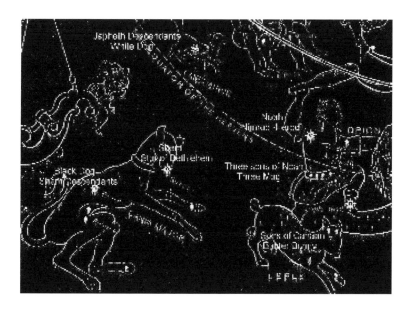

ORION

Orion is the great hunter. The three stars in his belt is easy to find. As the great hunter Orion would be Nimrod. The constellation also represents Noah after he debarks. In the New Testament, Orion is King Herod. The belt in Orion represents the three wise men who follow the Star of the East.

Orion is sometimes depicted as being headless. That would represent the attempted sacrifice of Isaac.

CANIS MAJOR

Sirius in the nose of Canis Major is the Star of the East. It was the star followed by the magi. In the Old Testament, Canis Major represents Shem and his descendents.

CANIS MINOR

Canis Minor is the constellation of Japheth and his descendents. It is also known as the "white dog."

LEPUS THE HARE

This is the constellation of the moon-hare, or Easter Bunny. The four stars of the constellation of Lepus the Hare, located in the subservient position at the footstool of Orion, would represent the sons of Canaan.

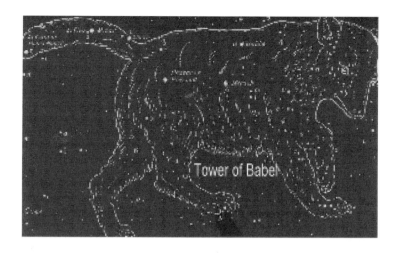

Tower of Babel

URSA MAJOR

Ursa Major (Big Dipper) is the Tower of Babel. It is located near the top of the heavens. The Tower was viewed as a step pyramid. During the night, as the earth rotated, the Tower would "overturn." The star Alioth, which has the same Arabic name as a star in Auriga is the marker of Rachel's burial location.

It is here, in Ursa Major, where Reuben took his father's concubine, Bilhah represented by the star Alcor.

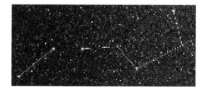

HERCULES

Hercules is Abraham. Abraham would be represented by the brightest star in the constellation, Ras Algethi, which is "the head of the kneeling man." This would be a later definition of the star. Its original Arab name was most likely Ras Kalb al Rāí, "the Shepherd's Dog. Sarah is linked to the star Kornephorus vel Rutilicus, which is perhaps the diminutive of rutilus, "golden red," or "glittering."

In the New Testament Hercules would be the resurrected Christ.

OPHIUCHUS AND SERPENS

Ophiuchus is typically depicted as a shepherd who struggles with a serpent (Serpens). This is the divided lands of Abraham and Lot. In ancient times Ophiuchus was seen as a large field. There is a line of stars that runs through it which was considered a boundary. This was the line drawn between the feuding shepherds of Abraham and Lot.

In the New Testament this would be the Potter's field where Judas (Serpens) killed himself. As a healer, Ophiuchus would represent Nicodemus.

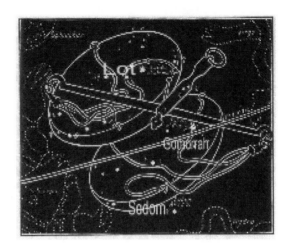

LIBRA

As the sign of the scales, Libra represents judgment. In this case it would the judgment of Sodom and Gomorrah. In the New Testament it would the trial of Christ. Centaurus is located just below this constellation.

CANCER

In Egypt, Cancer was the dung beetle, known as the scarab, which would ball up her small eggs inside balls of dung. They would grow and hatch in what would appear to be a spontaneous birth. From this action Cancer became the sign associated with barren births.

This is the sign of the barren births of Isaac, Esau, Jacob, and Samson. Coupled with Virgo, it was the sign of the virgin birth of Jesus.

At the center of Cancer is a cluster of stars known today as "The Beehive." In the Greek-Roman times it was called Praesepe and generally known as "The Manger" or "The Crib." This area was originally considered a rest stop or oasis and evolved into a manger or crib, which played out in the nativity scene of Christ.

Isaac's servant travels to Nahor, the root of which means "snorting or a nostril." This would be Praesepe, located in the head of the crab, between the claws.

Isaac's servant asks for a place to stay at the house of Rebekah's father and she offers him a bed of straw. This seemed acceptable and even comfortable in this age, unlike the humble stigmatism later attached to the similar accommodations offered to Mary at the birth of Jesus.

Rebecca will be the mother of Gemini, the twins Jacob and Esau. She is the star Acubens. The name Rebecca means "to clog by tying up the fetlock or fettering by beauty." In this case, Isaac was held by the beauty of Rebecca.

There are two stars in Cancer which represent the "Northern Ass" and the "Southern Ass." They are Asellus Boreas and Asellus Australis. One would be the ass rode by Mary. Ishmael, was a "a wild ass of a man" in Genesis 16:12 when fully translated. He would also be one of those stars.

Because of the lack of stars, Cancer was known as "The Dark Sign." This would make it the cave of the nativity as well as the cave where Lot had sex with his daughters.

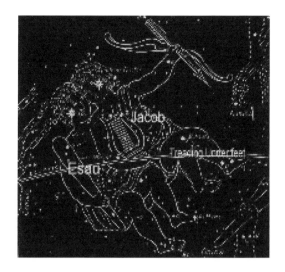

GEMINI

Gemini, the sign of the twins, are the twins Esau and Jacob. Esau, being the first born is on the left closest to Cancer. This sign is sometimes shown with the second twin inverted. This would put Jacob's head at Esau's heel. Jacob came out holding the heel of Esau.

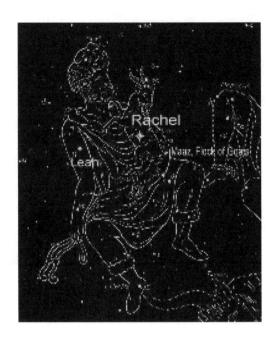

AURIGA

Auriga is the land to which Jacob flees. It is the sign of a Wagoner holding a goat. The brightest star in Auriga is Alioth or Capella, which means "she-goat." This is Rachel which means "she-sheep." Leah would be the star known as Haedi to the Latins. It was coupled with Capella, and together the Arabs knew them as Al Jadyain, "The Two Young He Goats." They were also known as "The Lambs."

Another star in Auriga is Maaz, which means "flock of goats." This would have been the sheep tended by Rachel. Later this would be the story of Jacob working for Laban—separating speckled and spotted goats as well as brown and white lambs.

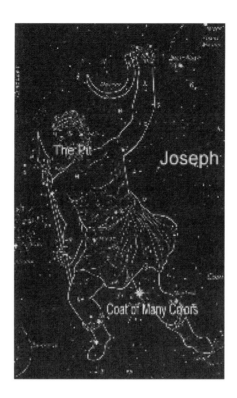

BOÖTES

The colorful garnet star Arcturus is the coat of many colors. In the New Testament, this star would represent the mock robe of Jesus. On the Euphrates, Arcturus is identified as "Shepherd of the Heavenly Flock." This is Joseph's role in Boötes.

NORTHERN CROWN

The Northern Crown represents the complex story of Judah and Tamar. This sign was associated with a maze, the color red, and string. The thread and maze is symbolically important. It represents the womb and umbilical cord. This was typical symbolism in ancient times.

Tamar had twins in a birth involving a bizarre scarlet thread, during which the second child came out first. One child stuck out his hand and a red thread was tied around it. Then the hand went back into Tamar. The child without the string became the first one out the birth canal.

In the New Testament this would be Jesus' crown of thorns.

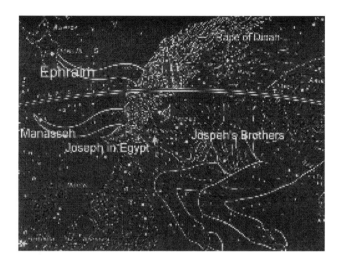

TAURUS

The generosity of Taurus is the generosity Joseph shows his brothers in Egypt. The two horns of Taurus represent the two his two sons, Ephraim and Manasseh. The Hyades are Joseph's brothers. Joseph would be the star Al Debaran.

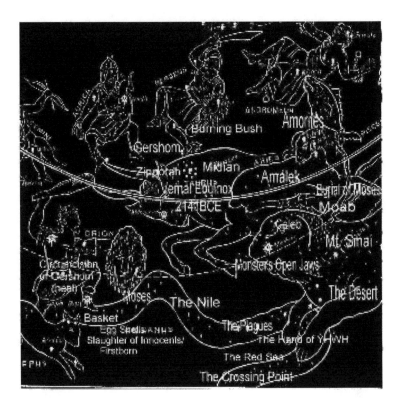

ERIDANUS RIVER

The Eridanus is the river of the heavens. It represents the Nile River in the story of Moses. The river starts at the foot of Orion. This is where a group of stars would represent the basket Moses was placed in as a child. One star outside of the basket represents the killing of new born. This would be the "slaughter of the innocents" in the Gospel of Matthew as well as the Passover in Egypt.

The Eridanus flows as the Nile, then turns into the Red Sea. The star at the end of the river represented the dry land where Moses crossed the Red Sea.

THE PLEIADES

The Pleiades is the seven sisters. Moses wife, Zipporah, was one of seven sisters. In Hebrew, Zipporah is literally translated as "bird or fowl." In Greek mythology the brightest star in the Pleiades was Celaeno, the wife of

Poseidon, the sea god. Moses parted the waters. Celaeno, in Greek mythology was also a name of a harpy, a bird like creature. In Ur, the Pleiades was represented by a bird on the back of Taurus. There was an ancient Babylonian city known as Sippara (phonetically similar to Zipporah). Its patron deity was Luagal-banda, "the divine storm bird" or Zu-bird. It was known to have given birth to Taurus and was associated with the Pleiades.

The Pleiades, along with Gemini comprised the story of the rape of Dinah.

PERSEUS

Perseus is Moses' son Gershom. The star Al Gol is a binary star, and its brightness changes a scale of two magnitudes over time and then dims. This would have seemed eerie to the ancients, who, in their imagination, made it into the head of Medusa. The Bible instead uses the "flickering" to turn it into the vocal "burning bush."

Perseus also represents Joseph fleeing from Potiphar's wife.

CETUS

Cetus is the wilderness. It is the forty years Moses spent wandering in the desert. It is the desert where Jesus spent his forty day fast. The head of Cetus was known as Al Kaff al Jidhmah, "the Part of the Hand", and was most the hand which pushed the Egyptians back. The star Mira represents Mt. Sinai. Mira is another star that oscillates like the burning bush. The distinction is that the naked eye can see it go from visible magnitudes to invisible magnitudes. It is located in the neck of Cetus. The star is garnet in color and is called the "south pole" of the Milky Way. Its title was "Wonderful Star." The appearance and disappearance of the star Mira would account for the odd instructions about having infrequent access to YHWH on Sinai. Sometimes YHWH would be on Mt. Sinai (Mira), and other times he would not be there, making sporadic appearances just like the star.

ARIES

Aries is the sign of war and victory. Great fighters are associated with Aries. When the Hebrews spied on Canaan they saw great fortified cities and fighters that were giants (Nephilim). The cities, as described, mirrored the layout of Aries. Amalek lived in the Negeb, or the "southland." This would be the flank of Aries where the star Al Botain is located. The name means "Little Belly," and it is associated astrologically with finding treasure and retaining captives.

The Hittites, Jebusites, and Amorites all live in the mountains or the head and horns of Aries. The Canaanites live by the sea and along the Jordan River. The sea and the Jordan River is Pisces. The leg of Aries passes through a stream which connects the two fish. One of the fish is located near the head of Aries. In the Denderah Zodiac, Aries is called Tametouris Ammon, which means "the reign, or government, of Ammon." In Syria it was Amroo. The head of Aries would be the home of the Amorites.

THE BAND

The Band represents the binding to one's enemies. In this case it was the Israelites intermingling with the Moabites.

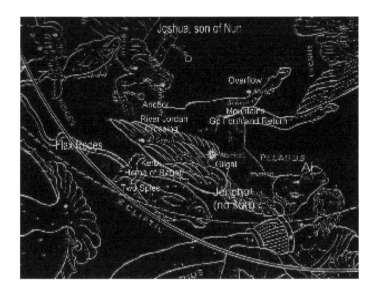

PISCES

If one was to ask several people to write a story involving the number two, fish, hiding, flax, and a sea monster; one would get a variety of stories which had the same basic elements. So it is with cosmic myth comparison.

In Greek mythology Pisces was associated with Venus and Cupid, who dove into the water for a swim. When the TWO encountered a SEA MONSTER they turned themselves into FISH to avoid the monster. In order not to lose each other in the water, they tied themselves together with a rope made of FLAX. They swam and HID from the monster. (Friday is the day that honors Venus, the goddess of love. Fish eaten on that day in her honor were considered an aphrodisiac. Lovemaking was done on Friday, also in her honor. Conflicts arose when Friday fell on the thirteenth. Thirteen was the number of the menstruation cycle because there are thirteen lunar months in a solar year. In several cultures it was taboo to make love during this time.)

The Bible has a story with the same elements, but is radically different. After Moses' story ends in Aries, the next zodiac constellation is Pisces and the next story is

29

that of Joshua sending his TWO spies into Jericho. Joshua is the son of Nun, which means FISH. They met Rahab, whose name means SEA MONSTER. When the authorities came to look for the spies she HID them in stalks of FLAX.

Venus as the goddess of love and Rahab being a prostitute both imply some sort of promiscuity. This would be a sixth point of convergence. What is interesting in this story is the fact the flax adds no real significance to the story except from an astrological viewpoint.

PEGASUS

Pegasus represents the first leg in the conquests of Joshua. The River Jordan flows along the base of Pegasus, who is partially in water. Jericho lacks a star because the city was destroyed and never rebuilt. Ai lies in the mouth region of Pegasus as the star, Enif or Al-Anf, which means "water," but was also called "the nose" or "the mouth" or "the lip." It was associated with "something steep" or "danger." In Joshua 7:5:

And the men of Ai smote of them about thirty and six men: for they chased them from before the gate even unto Shebarim, and smote them in the going down: wherefore the hearts of the people melted, and became as water.

Here in this one line we have all the elements of the star: water, danger, a steep precipice, and the gate as the mouth.

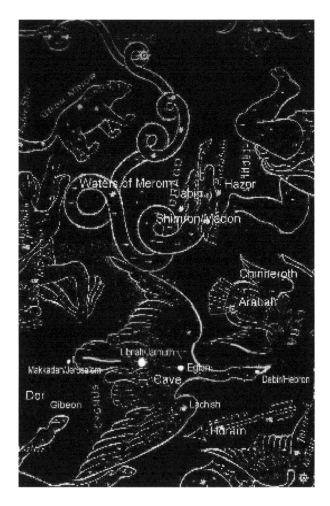

CYGNUS, THE SWAN

Gibeon, or "hill city," is the next adventure tale. This story involves the five kings and Joshua's memorable act in which he made the sun stand still for a day. Hills generally mean either being at the head of a constellation or going up (north) in the sky chart, as we have discovered. In this case, Gibeon would be a shared star between the constellations of Pegasus and Cygnus, Azelfafage. E. W. Bullinger divides it into two stars: Azel, "who goes and returns quickly," and Fafage, "the gloriously shining forth." In this case, Azel fits the case very nicely for Gibeon. The people from Gibeon pretended that they lived far away when they visited Joshua, whereas in reality they lived with them. Thus, when they visited, they went and returned quickly. Joshua made a pact to defend Gibeon from invaders. Once it was learned that Gibeon had made peace with Joshua, the five kings decided to attack.

The kings came from faraway places to attack Gibeon, only to be rained on by hailstones and then witness the sun standing still. The Greek legend of the constellation claims Phaethon, a mortal son of Helios, the sun god drives his father's sun chariot recklessly and threatens to destroy the earth.

The elements are the same. In the Greek legend we have a runaway sun in the sky and a shooting star, i.e., a hailstone from heaven. The Swan is seen as flying into the Milky Way. This area of the sky is bright and acted as a "second sun." This is where the sun stood still. Cygnus was the location of a supernova 15,000 years ago—which accounts for its nighttime brightness. This area of space would certainly have been far brighter 4000 years ago. This is where Joshua stopped the sun in the sky.

The five bright stars in Cygnus represents the five kings conquered by Joshua. The dark Cygnus Rift would represent the cave in which the kings were placed.

LYRA, THE HARP

Lyra, the "harp," represents the two kingdoms of the south, Chinneroth, which happens to mean "harp-shaped," and Arabah, which is "desert." Vega, the brightest in the constellation, is called "the vulture star." Vega would be Arabah and the star Sheliak, or "tortoise shell" or "lyre," would be Chinneroth, "the harp."

DRACO, THE DRAGON

The other attack group is to the north, or upper area of the sky. North of Lyra is the constellation Draco. Jabin, the king of Hazor, is the head of Draco. The author tells us that Hazor was at the head in Joshua 11:10:

32

And Joshua at that time turned back, and took Hazor, and smote the king thereof with the sword: for Hazor beforetime was the head of all those kingdoms.

The name Jabin means "he whom God observes." Alwaid is a star situated in the head of Draco, known also as "the Dragon's eye." In Hebrew it was Rastaban, "head of the subtle serpent."

Achshaph, the name of which means "to practice witchcraft," is a city located at the foot of Mt. Carmel. There is a general air of evil associated with the constellation Draco. The name of a third city, Shimron, means "watch-height," and Madon means "strife." Mizpah, another name mentioned, means "watchtower." Between the "he whom God observes" and all the references to high places, this must be a constellation near the top of the heavens. Four to five stars make up the head of Draco. These would be those cities.

The battle scene takes place at the waters of Merom, which means "high place." I would assume this to be the body of the snake, which looks like a river. Giansa, the name of a star located in the body of Draco, means "the Poison Place." Either here or at the place of Thuban, "the snake" (or "the dragon's tail") would be the place of the battle. Dor means "generation," "age," or "dwelling," is most likely the small constellation Equuleus. Kitalpha is the main star. Arabs called it Al Faras al Awwal, "the First Horse."

The significance of this battle may not be apparent. This will later represent Armageddon, as spoken of in both the Zend-Avesta and Revelation. This is when all the kingdoms of the north (Draco) will swoop down and attack Israel.

The book of Revelation, the Zend-Avesta, and the Norse myths all have their hell with their armies of their evil "satanic" enemies originating in the north (Draco) and moving southward to attack the chosen people. There is an element of truth to this, as many of Israel's enemies (Hittites, Greeks, and Romans, for example) originated to their north. They believed the stars told the story of Israel's past, present, and future. Linkages between the stars and

33

actual places, people, and events would be natural, as this was "God's plan."

CEPHEUS, THE KING

Abimelech, whose name means "my father is the king," went to Shechem, "the shoulder." Aldermin, a star in the shoulder of the king, means "right arm." It also signifies—along with Alphirk, in the belt—a "flock." This would correspond to the profuse number of Abimelech's siblings.

Judges 9:2 has an odd phrase:

Speak, I pray you, in the ears of all the men of Shechem, Whether is better for you, either that all the sons of Jerubbaal, which are threescore and ten persons, reign over you, or that one reign over you? remember also that I am your bone and your flesh.

"Speak…in the ears" is the odd phrase. This would be a reference to Erakis, a garnet star in the right ear of Cepheus. The garnet is of the color that implies deceitfulness. In this case, it is symbolizing the deceitfulness of Abimelech in using the money given to him by his brothers to hire mercenaries to kill them.

Al Rai, a star in the knee of Cepheus, according to Bullinger, means "[he] who bruises or breaks." This would describe the murder of the siblings. Jotham, whose name means "YHWH is perfect," was spared because he hid in the foot of Cepheus—which also happens to be a star shared with Ursa Minor, namely Polaris.

Abimelech gathered the citizens at the "oak of the pillar" in Shechem with the entire house of Millo ("rampart mound"). This oak is the staff Cepheus holds in his right hand.

Abimelech conquers a number of cities which have towers and then has his skull crushed by a woman with a millstone—apparently having stood too close to a fortified wall. God has his revenge for Abimelech's wrongdoing and Jotham returns to the people.

The action essentially takes place in the same location using previously discussed stars. However, now things go the other way, and Abimelech loses his life in Judges 9:57:

And all the evil of the men of Shechem did God render upon their heads: and upon them came the curse of Jotham the son of Jerubbaal.

Literally this should be "and God brought them back on their heads." What is at play here is a description of the movement of Cepheus, Ursa Minor, and Cassiopeia in relation to the heavens. As the nighttime sky turns, Cepheus and Cassiopeia become inverted or turned upside down. In this case, all the high towers (stars near the top) fall relative to their constellation figure. When Cepheus is on his head, Jotham, who is Polaris in the foot of Cepheus, stands over him. Cepheus is on his head, presumably having his skull cracked open by Cassiopeia with a millstone.

CASSIOPEIA

Millo mentioned above, would be Caph, a nearby star in the constellation Cassiopeia. Caph is located in the throne of "the queen." Al Tizini designated the star as Al Sanam al Nakah, "the Camel's Hump."

URSA MINOR

Jotham spoke to the people from Mount Gerizim. Notice that Abimelech is associated with a mound and Jotham with a mount. In Judges 9:7, Jotham speaks from Polaris in Ursa Minor:

And when they told it to Jotham, he went and stood in the top of Mount Gerizim, and lifted up his voice, and cried, and said unto them, Hearken unto me, ye men of Shechem, that God may hearken unto you.

Jephthah's Daughter

ANDROMEDA

At this point the author takes us to the crises in Ammon. Jephthah is brought back from exile to battle the children of Ammon, who have crossed over the River Jordan (Pegasus) to battle against the Israelites. Ammon is in Gilead, a rocky region. This would point to Cassiopeia/Andromeda. Jephthah, disinherited because he was the son of a prostitute, now returns to lead the army. He promises God that, if he is successful in his quest, he will sacrifice to him the first thing he sees upon his return. As fate would have it, Jephthah sees his daughter first. He then sacrifices her after giving her two months to lament her virginity. Astrologically, Andromeda is linked to "purity of thought." Similarly, the virgin is linked to purity.

Andromeda is pictured with chains. Jephthah's daughter is wearing tambourines or trimbrels, and she dances.

Andromeda is a constellation associated with preparation for spring. The sacrifice of the virgin or end of virginity is symbolic of the opening of the spring. Jephthah's daughter spends two winter months lamenting about her virginity.

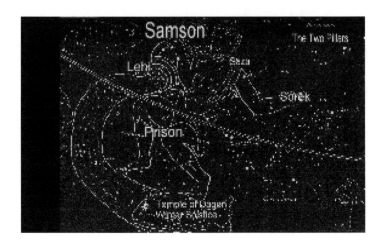

AQUARIUS/ DELPHINUS/ PISCES AUSTRALIS

In Aquarius, Samson grabbed the fresh jawbone of an ass and killed a thousand men, then thirsted. He took the jawbone, cast it away, and then God opened up the earth and water came out. This takes place at the stars Lehi ("jaw"), Ramat-Lehi ("height of jawbone"), and Enhakkore ("eye or spirit of one calling"). The place where the spring of water gushed forth is easy to figure out: it is the urn in Aquarius which spills the water. Aquarius was sometimes depicted as an ass carrying two urns of water.

Samson now heads for Gaza ("strong, mighty, fierce") to see a prostitute. He is at the gates of Gaza in the star Sadalsuud, located in the left shoulder of Aquarius. The star is called "Luck of Lucks," the star of mighty destiny. It symbolizes the rising of the sun and the passing of winter. It was here the Philistines set an ambush for Samson. They waited all night for him at the city gate and said they would kill him at morning light. Samson slept until midnight and then got up. He took the hold of the doors to the city gate, along with the two door posts, placed them on his shoulders, and carried them up to the top of the mountain that faces Hebron. Hebron is in Cygnus. Going up from Aquarius is the constellation Delphinus, "the Dolphin," which is facing Cygnus.

40

The two pillars would later represent the polar axis around which the constellations turn. Some early Christian sects (Nestorians, Melkites) considered the constellation as the "cross of Jesus." This is evidence that they knew the cosmic myth of the Old Testament. The pillars carried by Samson would be represented by the same constellation as the cross carried by Jesus. Simon of Cyrene also carried this cross for Jesus. Coincidently, it was Eratosthenes (273–192 BCE) of Cyrene who, at the town of Cyrene, correctly determined the diameter and size of the Earth.

Samson then goes to the *wadi* Sorek. A *wadi* is a dry desert valley awaiting the spring rains. Sorek means "choice wine or grapes." This would be yet another star in Aquarius, Albali. The star is the "swallower," as the desert swallows water. It got its name because this star seems to swallow the light of two brighter stars

Delilah has a barber cut off Samson's hair. Samson's eyes are put out: therefore, he loses his strength at the winter solstice, the only time when the Philistines can dominate him. He is placed in a prison house. I would suggest that the prison house is Skat, "the star of the foundation."

Samson's hair, like the sun, returns. During the Philistine feast to their god Dagon, Samson kills 3,000 Philistines on the roof of the temple by taking down the two middle pillars (poles of the winter and summer solstice). The temple is the star Fomalhaut, the ancient star designating the winter solstice. The constellation of the Pisces Australis was also associated with the fish-god Dagon.

CAPRICORN

This is the story of David and Goliath. David was in the tail of Capricorn. He was the star Nashira. The fish tail of Capricorn represented Israel as a possible extension of Pisces the fish. The head of the goat was to be sacrificed as atonement. Goliath represented that sacrifice. Nashira represented "the bringer of good tidings." Goliath appeared in the head of Capricorn as the star(s) Dabih and Geida Prima. The Arabic name for Dabih is Sa'd adh-dhabih, "the Lucky One of the slaughterer." The Arabs would make a sacrifice at the helical rising of this star to aid with the return of captives.

The opposing camps were both atop mountains. The two met for battle in the valley between the head of the goat and tail of the fish. Castra, a star in the belly of Capricorn, depicted Goliath. The name Castra refers to a military fortress associated with an uncontrollable temper and destruction. It was the massive armor of Goliath.

42

SAGITTA

Saul throws a spear or javelin at David and misses. This would be the constellation Sagitta, "the arrow."

AQUILA

David goes to Samuel at Ramah ("hill") and relates to Samuel what has transpired between him and Saul. When we see the word "hill," we are sometimes directed to a constellation just above the zodiac, as was Auriga. In this case, we are dealing with Aquila the eagle. Naioth, a place in Ramah, is the place of the prophets. As a prophet, Samuel represents the eyes of God. In ancient Egypt and Babylon, Aquila was "the Living Eye." Hence, we get the "place of the prophets." Saul goes to a big cistern in Sechu ("watch tower"). This would be the eye of the eagle which soars high and watches the Earth. The "cistern" would imply a dark space, and indeed Aquila is full of dark nebulae, although none are currently visible to the naked eye. They are faint and can be seen with binoculars. It is possible that the nebulas were visible 4,000 years ago.

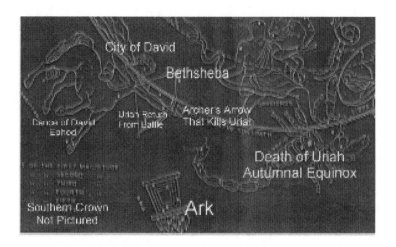

SAGITTARIUS/ARA/ SCORPIO

David enters Sagittarius at the star Albalduh (located in the head). It is not a particularly bright star, but it occupies a large starless gap between the horns of Capricorn and the head of Sagittarius. The star was known as "the city" or "the district" and was associated with building. Albalduh was the City of David, the stronghold surrounded by empty space.

I find this passage interesting, since it was said that the blind and lame feared David because his generosity was not for them. This is a characteristic of Sagittarius, whose generosity was for the rich. This is evidenced in 2 Samuel 5:6:

And the king and his men went to Jerusalem against the Jebusites, the inhabitants of the land, who spoke to David, saying, "You shall not come in here; but the blind and the lame will repel you," thinking, "David cannot come in here."

Sagittarius displayed the qualities of David, who was both poet and soldier. And as seen above, he was someone whose charity was not for the blind and lame. Sagittarius charity is for the rich and the arts.

David gathered his men to retrieve the Ark. This is fairly simple and straightforward. They went to "bring up" the Ark. Southeast of Sagittarius is the constellation Ara, or Ark. It is an altar which dwells between Scorpio and Aquarius. They had only gone six paces with the Ark when David danced in his "ephod." This would be the left leg of Sagittarius, At eventide, David went to the roof of his house and saw Bethsheba bathing. David lay with her as her husband while Uriah was away fighting in a war. David called Uriah back from battle and asked him to go lie ("wash his feet") with his wife. Uriah did not. Knowing Bethsheba was with his child and trying to avoid a sexual scandal, David had Uriah killed—apparently with an arrow—by placing him at the front of the battle.

This scene represents the bow of Sagittarius. David is on the roof of his house. This places him in the head of Sagittarius.

Bethsheba is the star at the north end of the bow of Sagittarius, and by no coincidence is where the head of Sagittarius (David) is facing. Kaus Boreal—along with the star Polis—formed the Akkadian Anu-ni-tum, said to have been associated with the great goddess Ishtar.

The living Uriah is represented by the bow. These stars are associated with the coming and going from the Milky Way. For that reason, David has Uriah return home and then sends him out again.

Uriah is then placed in front of the point of the arrow, Kaus Medius, where he is killed in Antares, the heart of Scorpio. This is where Sagittarius is aiming his arrow. Antares means "Rival of Mars." Both David and Uriah were known as warriors.

SOUTHERN CROWN

This is the crown of Solomon.

JESUS

The cosmic tale did not stop with David. It continued onward. Psalms, Isaiah, Daniel, Ezekiel, and Job all have overt astrological references. The explanations of the stories as given in the midrashim proved that the priesthood still knew the exact meaning of the cosmic connection within their text well into the second century CE, and perhaps the Middle Ages. The Jewish *Pseudepigrapha* and the Dead Sea Scrolls also had astrological references. In the New Testament, Revelation is an astrologer's dream. The book of Matthew was said to have been written for a Jewish audience. It also contains the most astrological references of the four Gospels.

The construction of the story of Jesus differs from the Old Testament. The story of Jesus started with only a partial cosmic myth—the passion—if we assume Mark was the earliest text. Numerous sayings and parables unrelated to any cosmic myth are included in this early manuscript. What we see in Matthew is the layering of the cosmic story on top of an existing text.

Another difference is that the equinoxes have progressed from the original Old Testament text. These should seem more familiar to us, with the vernal equinox in Aries, the autumnal equinox in Libra, and the summer and winter solstices in Cancer and Capricorn, respectively. There is no progression to new signs to add to the confusion of the text, although aspects of the ancient ordinances are still used.

Jesus' winter-solstice birth is depicted in the summer constellations and his spring passion is depicted in the autumn constellations—constellations seen just before sunrise at the winter solstice and vernal equinox.

From our previous study, it should be fairly simple for nearly anyone to identify the cosmic-myth aspects of the story. What follows is my interpretation of the cosmic myth of Jesus as presented in Matthew.

The Gospel of Matthew in the Stars

Chapter 1 of Matthew starts with the genealogy of Joseph. It incorporates Abraham, Isaac, Jacob, Judah and Tamar, and David and Solomon. This should not seem unusual. The text does refer to Joseph as "son of David." This shows a significant relationship. The messiah was to come from the "house of David." As the "son of David," this would connect Joseph to a solar sign, in this case Leo, the consort of Virgo, the virgin who can only be Mary.

Mary is the celestial Virgo. This fact is recognized unofficially by the Catholic Church in its celebration of the Immaculate Conception of Mary and her Assumption, as the dates are associated with ancient Roman rites involving Virgo. The virgin bringing forth a son would be the constellation Coma, which was depicted as the virgin with a child.

Chapter 2 of Matthew deals very heavily with the cosmic myth. This chapter is the sole reference for Herod's "slaughter of the innocents."

Bethlehem, the birthplace of Jesus, is literally translated as "house of bread." The word house can also be a zodiac constellation reference. Judging from ancient history, each house or clan was represented by a constellation. This custom dates from ancient Babylon, third millennium BCE. In this case, the "house of bread" would be Virgo, which was associated with wheat.

The author wanted us to associate Jesus with the summer solstice. With the addition of July and August to the calendar, the breakup of Asad would have been finalized—thus separating Libra, Virgo, Leo, and Cancer once and for all. It would seem the author is of the "old school," inasmuch as he maintains a relationship of Virgo with the summer solstice. Jesus is called a "Nazarene," as was Samson. Again, this is a representation of the long hair associated with the solar aspect.

The "slaughter of the innocents" by Herod is very similar to the midrash of the "slaughter of the innocents" by Nimrod, in Abraham's tale. The Hebrews associated Nimrod with Orion. Herod fits Orion.

The three wise men that follow the "Star of the East" would represent the three stars of the belt of Orion which follow Sirius ("Chieftain of the East") across the sky. The three wise men replace the three sons of Noah. In modern representations one of the wise men is typically given dark skin, as if to represent the three races of man, as did the three sons of Noah. The ox and lamb in the modern nativity scene are a throwback to 2000 BCE, when the vernal equinox changed from Taurus (ox) to Aries (lamb). The ass would suggest an association with the stars of Cancer that represents the Northern and Southern Ass. The prophecy that pictures the messiah riding into Jerusalem on an ass would indicate an association with a solar deity, just as the asses of Cancer are associated with the summer solstice.

The "innocents," or murdered children, could be represented by Lepus at the foot of Orion. It is also possible that they could be linked to the same star in Eridanus, which represented the murder of the firstborn in the tale of Moses. This would accord with the fact that the Holy Trio fled to Egypt and then returned—another Eridanus representation.

There is an odd statement about Rachel's weeping for her children in Rama. Rama literally means "hill," and Rachel was born in Auriga—an area associated with a hill.

From chapter 3 until the Passion Story, the text lacks any real connection to the cosmic tale other than the beheading of John the Baptist. The associations are loose, and the lack of continuity may mean they are merely coincidental. In chapter 3 the "wilderness" is typically Cetus, and the Jordan River would be in Pegasus. If we connect the dove to the story of Noah, then this watery baptism would best fit into Argo.

In chapter 4, Jesus' sojourn in the wilderness is for forty days. This can take place astrologically only in Cetus. This is the wilderness Moses transverses for forty years. The mountain Jesus goes up onto would be the star *Mira*, which in the Old Testament corresponded to Mt. Sinai. Jesus meets Peter and Andrew—generally associated with Pisces because of their occupation as fishermen. Furthermore, the chapter mentions the lands of Zebulon (Pisces) and Nephthalim (Sagittarius).

Chapters 5 and 6 contain Jesus' Sermon on the Mount. The most natural correspondence would be with Polaris in Ursa Minor where Jotham gave his speech. In chapter 7, Jesus tells us to "judge not," which is a possible reference to Pleiades . When he speaks of "thy brother's eye," this would be the eye of Taurus, as it was with Joseph. Likewise, the sermon on alms giving is a further reference to the generosity of Taurus, recalling its association with the beginning of the rainy season.

Chapter 8 of Matthew presents us with a Roman centurion. The soldier would typically point us to Aries. Jesus mentions the Triad of Abraham, Isaac, and Jacob. The tempest sea and the swine that perish in the water are most likely images evoking Eridanus.

Jesus is now in his own city. I would reckon this to be Pisces or Cygnus; it also could be Sagittarius. Matthew does a turnabout. He was sitting as a tax collector, then arose and followed Jesus. This would be the turnabout of the constellation of Cepheus. The two blind men who are bound to the devil would correspond to the binding of the Band in Pisces. (The Band was discussed in regard to Moses and the Moabites, associated more with Aries in that era.)

Chapters 10–13 are very trivial in regard to any cosmic-myth significance. A possible reference would be to Pegasus, as when Jesus commands the apostles to go to the lost sheep of Israel and then return. When Jesus teaches and preaches in the cities of the disciples, he could be almost anywhere in the constellation group bounded by Pisces, Pegasus, and Cygnus. Jesus, on being accused of being Satan, would most likely be Draco. The scene by the rocky shore may have taken place in Andromeda.

In chapter 14, the midway point, is where we find the description of the decapitation of John the Baptist. The decapitation would be the winter solstice. This is a definite reference to Capricorn, which has the beheading of Goliath. Jesus then feeds the multitude with two fishes (unmistakably Pisces) and five loaves of bread (Cygnus, perhaps). The "Land of Gennesaret" literally means "the land of the harp," thus makes this Lyra.

49

In chapter 15, there is a woman on a coast with a vexed daughter. This would be Cassiopeia/Andromeda. In chapter 16, Jesus gives his "take up the cross" speech, which is most likely a Delphinus (Northern Cross) reference. The "vision on the mount" in chapter 17 is most likely Aquila, the constellation of prophecy. Chapter 19 mentions eunuchs and the suffering of little children. Both references would be to Orion. In chapter 20, "the first shall be last" and "the last shall be first" would be a reference to Cepheus.

In chapter 21, Jesus enters the City of David—a location identified with Sagittarius. The temple incident would be representative of Ara. The prophecies in chapters 24 and 25 would be of Aquila. This is the point at which Jesus takes on the persona of David.

Chapter 26 begins a story with some very distinct cosmic references. Jesus is being attended to by a woman in Bethany. Bethany means "house of misery." This would be a reference to Scorpio and its stinger. The conspiracy and treachery to capture Jesus, along with Judas's kiss, would be Hydra, "the serpent." Jesus' praying in the garden would be an Eden reference; hence, also a reference to Leo/Virgo. The cup of the Last Supper is easily identified as Crater, "the cup," both of which are said to give wisdom. The crowing of the cock is a phallic symbol relating to the sun. This would be either a Leo or a Cancer reference.

The next chapter is likewise filled with cosmic references. The Potter's Field would be the ancient field of Ophiuchus, "the healer" or "the snake-holder," with the repented Judas as Serpens. The trial and the two choices of Jesus or Barabbas would be stereotypically Libra, "the scales of judgment." The name Pilate means "armed with a spear"; this is a natural allusion to Centaurus, killing his victim with spear in hand.

The mocking of Jesus is the same as the torment of Joseph in Boötes, complete with the garnet robe (coat of many colors) in the role of Arcturus. The bloody crown of thorns would be the scarlet color associated with the Corona Borealis. Simon of Cyrene, carrying the cross, is once again Delphinus, the Northern Cross. The crucified

Jesus is Lupus, and his cross is most likely an early version of the Southern Cross. The earthquake at the death of Jesus is the same as the earthquake at the death of Abel, who was also Lupus. Joseph of Arimathea—who tends to the body—would be Ophiuchus, as "the healer."

In chapter 28, we have the two Mary's—demonstrating the dual nature of Virgo. Hercules would be the likely association with the resurrected Jesus.

CONCLUSION

There are many stories in the Bible that are not told in the stars. Attempting to place them there would be wrong. For instance, other than the crown, Solomon is not represented in the stars. If you want to know more about how stories were matched up to the stars, please examine *On Earth as it is in Heaven, The Cosmic Roots of the Bible.*

The fact that scripture is depicted in the stars does not in any way prove or disprove the Bible. It only demonstrates there is a correlation between the two.

Made in the USA
Coppell, TX
06 December 2023

25183644R00031